Two Gulls, One Hawk

Two Gulls, One Hawk

James Hoggard

Prickly Pear
Press

1983

Grateful acknowledgment is made by the author to the National Endowment for the Arts for a creative writing fellowship grant.

Prickly Pear Press
2132 Edwin St.
Fort Worth, Texas
76110

Contents

Foreword

James Hoggard's *Two Gulls, One Hawk,* the tenth book from Prickly Pear Press in ten years, represents a milestone for those of us associated with an imprint that has issued collections accounting in part for a Dobie Paisano Fellowship and the poet laureateship of Texas for 1982, as well as publishing with Studia Hispanica Editors the award-winning bilingual anthology, *Washing the Cow's Skull.* Beginning in 1973, Prickly Pear released two chapbooks and its first anthology, *The New Breed,* in which Hoggard and twenty-four other contributors connected with the state first appeared in a publication devoted to the new Texas poetry. In several ways, this tenth book reflects the fulfillment of *The New Breed's* promise, at the same time that it returns us to the gropings in the creative dark those poets were experiencing more than a decade ago.

With the title poem of this volume, James Hoggard has achieved a long, dialectical piece that is unique in Texas letters. And while it is the authentic expression of a native poet, "Two Gulls, One Hawk" draws upon a wide range of biblical, classical, mystical, and Southwestern strains in building up and counterpointing its themes of family love, a sense of place, and the creative act. Weaving his motifs and images—of sticks, snakes, birds, the weather, grasshoppers, miracles, and human ties—Hoggard presents a warp and woof that is at once Southwestern and Greek, prophetic and poetic, contemporary and classic. The poem's alternating voices are rich with linguistic play and moving in their emotional responses one to the other. Much of the work's multilevel impact is owing to the poet's skillful manipulation of his image and motivic patterns in a poetic line that is his alone. As a poem that concerns husband-wife and father-son relationships, it is the work of a mature artist who has come to sing of universals in a local idiom that includes the lowly sights and sounds of mesquite and cicada.

On the other hand, "Tornado's Eye" is a poem that recalls the poet's origins, his early journey into the caves of mystery and meaning. In his search for a self-image, the boy in Hoggard's autobiographical piece stumbles over one impression after another, only vaguely aware of a trail that will eventually lead him to poetic invention. The awkwardness of the youth is paralleled by the poem's fumbling effort to discover a voice and a means of recording the significance inherent in the poet's past. Even though such an interpretation constitutes a pathetic fallacy, "Tornado's Eye" serves nonetheless as an important complement to the title poem—the one revealing Hoggard's struggle to create a viable and vital art, the other paying witness to the fact that the poet has, as D. H. Lawrence proclaimed, "come through." Without the first there is not the second, and to have them both is evidence of the necessary ground that has been covered, not only by James Hoggard but by other Texas poets of a generation that promised much and has now delivered.

Prickly Pear Press, then, is proud, on the occasion of the tenth anniversary of its inception, to offer this testament of the strides made in Texas poetry by another writer who has breathed life into a people and place he long since accepted as his own.

Dave Oliphant

Tornado's Eye

1

Tall brush pulled back,
the cave's mouth gaped

mutely now I think
as if the secrets buried
in the Indian mound nearby
had astonished even
the sandstone hill

Stooping, we crawled inside
its gullet: huge room
lifting my 12-year-old eyes
so high my feet felt
they'd leave the rock-rough ground

I was entering that
which I didn't understand
and though my mind
seethed with lust
my groin was dumb

We went farther
The sharp coolness
turned dank
as if a giant's turd
had not yet died to stone

The vast place still,
no dust slapped
grit on sweating face
as hot winds had
in the mesquite pasture's scorch
we'd maneuvered through
to get our blown selves here

Boulders pinched the pathway
Halls led left and ahead
Flashlights went on
though sunlight poured
from a hole in the roof
forty feet up. We'd gone
deeper than I'd thought

it wasn't a journey through womb
but a wandering into daydarkness

Until I saw the million bats
hanging from the ceiling
like brown egg cups
I thought, Here's a place where
I could learn how to mate
if one of the college girls
would join me

Two months before
I'd taken my girlfriend
into a crypt back in town
in the Catholic graveyard

Ignoring the fecal air,
we sat on a slab,
talked about school,
ate Eskimo Pies

I was too shy to kiss her
and the next year
she ran off for marriage,
the little tart,
not even pregnant,
just whirling with hell

Feet slipping,
we scrimmaged for balance,
palms and fingers rubbed raw
on slick, sharp rock
A spring leaked
down the shiny walls

We slopped through a puddle,
found benches in rock
and listened to the teacher
tell us how
to recognize vampires:

those large bats
threading the dome
in circular flight

The stories were right
They don't sleep
when the others do,
but they won't get close
as long as you move

That night we hunted
for ringtail cats,
saw muskrats in a lagoon

If I'd only brought my frog-gigger
I could've left this bunch
and in the morning
caught crawdads, too
and lazed in a tank,
dreaming about diamondbacks' coils,
their heads in shade:
silhouettes of my big-toes

but that night we slept
in a plowed field
whose clods made the slow night long

The sandwich I'd brought
for breakfast was stale
and I threw it away
with the one packed for lunch

Then again we went
back in the cave,
crawled deeper than before
but all I brought back
was a bat

I kept it in a Mason jar
three days till it died
then buried it with coffee grounds
to keep the earth from turning rank
but never lost the biting taste
of day-old Miracle Whip
or the stiffness in my back,
the sickness in my gut
from trying to sleep
on hard, lumpy ground
or the softness on my eyes
of the pale swell of breast
I saw through a blouse
before I became
too worn out to care
that I in my ignorance
was making a journey

into what I still am not
even sure was self

> at the end of the breast is a bud
> the size of a berry
> and between the legs
> shrimp-scented hair

4

2

Six years before
in a damper, green place
where few winds blew,
I was tramp of the park next door

and at dusk one evening
before lightning bugs rose
I saw the neighborhood
watching a man
beat up a woman
until Bobby Boggs' father
chased the sleeveless undershirt off,
Bobby and his mother both crying,
hysterical Mr. Boggs'd get knifed

World War II just one year past
but something more than fighting
was going on between those two
They'd been necking
before the crowd arrived—
I'd heard her refuse
to go with him in the john
so he hit her
then pushed her down
and rode her waist
*   (yippi ti yay ti yo)*
while they cussed each other,
tried choking each other
there in the clearing
persimmon trees ringed

and the horse apples looked like cannonballs

The public john was a two-doored bunker,
playpen for us kids
We'd trade with girls there
touches on our underwear
and laugh while we squeezed
ripe persimmons in our hands

The next day Bobby and I and Nan

after checking the pipes
we kept in the creek
for catfish and crawdads

went under the Beckley St. bridge

As Nan pulled her shift off
Bobby told her, "One day you'll have big ones"
"And we'll all," she said, "have hair"

Laughing, Bobby asked me,
as he rubbed her mosquito-bite nipples,
"Don't you think she'll have great big ones?"

I couldn't tell
Her ninners looked just like ours

Cars were passing overhead
Bobby took a crap
then Nan squatted
to show us how she peed

A watersnake slid
through the weeds near
where our footprints were

was thinking of Henry Noble,
the gangster-gambler who lived down the street
Seven attempts had been made on his life
They'd get him on the ninth

That in Trinity Heights in Oak Cliff in Dallas
whose wet air turned
the bones in your legs
to sponge

and before I returned
to the place of my birth
where summersun's razorblades
sliced beneath skin
and a cave was required
in the mind to protect
yourself from the blast
of drouth in your bones

3

One morning my brother
threw a greasy cardboard
on a girl showing off
her Easter dress

She ran home crying
Cackling, Chuck slid down the slope
but Betty's mother came running
Grabbing us, she bawled us out
while Chuck in his white nightshirt
hunkered behind a big tree-stump
and laughed while the harpy
shook Bobby and me
loose from our skin
Scratched with terror,
we kept crying, "Lady!
We haven't, lady, done anything!"
but the hail of her voice
stormed upon us

and when we sold lemonade
our customers complained
it was sour and weak

"Short on sugar, long on water
You kids botched it this time,
and where in the world's the ice?"

but between sales we flooded
tarantulas out of their holes
and captured them in fruit jars
although we knew they could jump
twenty feet high
straight for the throat
and squirt poison in your eyes

I learned to ride a bicycle
after Bobby won one
in a drawing at the show

9

the number I had wasn't close
I didn't even have a number
In fact, I skipped that Saturday's show
I didn't like Johnny Mack Brown
   or Red Ryder either
   and the Bowery Boys were Yankees
   I figured their parents
   were Church of Christ
   You could tell by the blankness
   in Huntz and Leo's eyes

Nancy, too, was C of C
but Bobby was Catholic
and I a Methodist preacher's son
who argued that Jesus wasn't God
although I whipped Bobby good once
for claiming, "The Easter Bunny's a lie"

Then I got my bike,
its horn worked for a week,
and we pushed our world's edge back
when we weren't charging each other
in chickie-runs

We stole a pack of Camels and matches
from a parked pick-up,
pedaled toward a turn in the creek
near Chalk Hill where the waterfall was,
blocks away from home

but somehow Chuck arrived

   emerged from the brush
   in his white nightshirt

We lit up and smoked
and quickly turned grey,
all of us retching
or writhing in mud
sorry we couldn't even drown

except for Chuck
who couldn't get his lit

He looked like a pigmy ghost
Three years old, he'd poke
a cigarette into his mouth,
hold a match up at it

the wind would blow it out
or his own milk-breath

and he'd flip his weed
into the creek,
bum another one,
insisting we give him this time
a reefer that worked

little dead torpedoes
floating in the pool
by his dirty bare feet

Recovering, we tried to teach him
how to inhale

he needed to learn
to get sick, too

Striking a match
he threw away another butt
"It's broken," he said

and toddled off into the woods
where copperheads were

but when he got home
God or the thrust of our wishes
got him for being so smart

Mother opened his scalp
with a tin airplane's wing
she was tossing toward a box

Bringing him home
from the doctor she slammed
the cardoor on his hand
and raced him back
for another set of stitches

"Witches," she mumbled in tears, "witches"

while I, trying to imagine
the taste of broccoli,
sat with a puzzle
at the kitchen table

and before dessert one night
unscrewed the light
from our humming Frigidaire,
stuck my finger in the socket
to see what the current did
with the little bulb gone

I felt the shock till morning

4

We moved to Greenville
when my father was named
District Superintendent

I later found out
too late to strut about it
he was youngest in the history
of the North Texas Conference

THE BLACKEST LAND
THE WHITEST PEOPLE
the hanging sign on the main street said

one day it fell
on the hood of a car
outside Ernie's
 sawdust-floored barbecue place
 near the depot
 where Thursday nights
 the cook for the train
 leaned out the window and dropped us
 warm sacks of cinnamon rolls

I learned to swim
by refusing to sink
and began going off the highboard,
did a dive I called a gainer
and convinced some kids
it was fun, but one
had to be rescued,
and I had severe pains, too,
after bellybusting three times
from a mile in the air

Exploring the town at 5 a.m.
on my Rocket Flyer bike

and hot to help
the silent sun rise
I talked to it, sang,
and later in the day,
for fifteen years more,
I might hear it
call me by name

A dead perch in the street one morning

white bellied,
a bloody wound
under its lip,
the body beginning
to pull away
from its scales,
its mouth said O

that fish became
an image I kept
later wondering if
it could have been
Osiris' lost member

5

During lunch hour, school days

I always ate at home
but got back with
time left to play
near the quonset hut
off the cement court

I began boxing

Duane Brown had got two sets
of Everlast gloves for Christmas

I was going to be heavyweight champ of the world
and travel in glory to Dallas
for the Golden Gloves

"The Old Scotchman," Gordon McClendon,
was whipping me up
with his re-creations of
turn-of-the-century fights
round by brilliant round

I thought they were real

They were real
for the truth's a gift
God gave us to play with
*   thus saith* (I wished) *the Lord*

and I had a hundred heroes
but Gentleman Jim Jeffries was king
though at night Caruso came close
when Mother and Daddy played opera,
each 45 record lasting
the length of a championship round

I took on all comers
except Terry Warren,
best of the school in art—
I didn't think I could whip him—
so told him he was too good a friend
for me to hit, and kept quiet
when I was around him
about the rumors of hammers
in my thundering left fist

and one day when
our class said poems
I recited in Braid Scott John 3:16-21

I'd found the passage on a card
soiling one morning in a gutter

The class and teacher looked perturbed
as if globs of hot oat meal
were drooling off my tongue

and sitting down I remembered
how during his book report the year before
Newman Peters had cupped his peter,
kept talking as his piddle dribbled
in a puddle on the hardwood floor

I was next
and stretching my right leg out
as far as it would go,
stepped over the pool of pee

Miss Tolleson said, "That's mean"

She didn't act glad to see me either
when I saw her next year
near the freakshows at the State Fair

Years later I thought about her
when I waited for a red light to change
and saw in my rearview mirror
a fine-feathered woman in elegant clothes
picking her nose

She saw me then jumped
but quickly had the finger
primping her eyebrows and ears

Maybe she hadn't been picking her nose
That finger had been
so far up her nostril
she could've been scratching
the backs of her eyes

6

Fourth grader, I played tackle
on the sixth grade football team
but was planning to be
the greatest fullback the nation had seen
and alerter than Bronco Nagurski
who knocked himself out
ramming his head into goalposts

I'd read about him and Niles Kinnick,
George Washington, too,
Alexander the Great,
Beethoven and Canute, Paderewski
and everybody else—
I shook Doak Walker's hand
and speaking my name
he asked how my folks were
and if Greenville was fine

I even composed music
though it didn't make sense
except when Mother played it—
  the music teacher
  said it was noise—

and sometimes,
because hotshot cowboys in movies did,
tried going to sleep in my clothes
but my parents thought that silly
and refused to let me
when they'd catch me

So then to find out
what others were like
I'd stand on the corner
and try hard to push
my soul up out of my body
on into whoever passed by

not so much to see
what the world looked like
from the angle where they stood
but to find how it felt
not to be me, to be them

but I never succeeded
though I'd been trying
from the age of five

and my brother no help
He mostly played by himself

He didn't seem to care
about the mysteries
in strangers and friends
He had his toy soldiers and battles
and a headful of facts
you could sometimes get him to say
when the winds in his dreams
blew for a while your way

7

We moved again,
this time to Wichita Falls

I was glad,
they had just won State
and in two years Greenville
had lost every game

The parsonage was being redone
We lived half that summer downtown

> *halls and stairwells to explore*
> *new people every day*
> *hot pavement, shady awnings*
> *and stores to wander through*
> *and people picking us up*
> *carting us off to swim and play*

> *all those rooms and all those floors*
> *but disappointment, too*

> *I never once saw*
> *any naked ladies*
> *behind the opened doors*
> *I'd peer into*

But running off my tongue
was *Dern y'm te kwa she,*
the opening phrases of
"Bringing In The Sheaves"

> *my class had learned it years before*
> *from a missionary who*
> *had a furlough from China*

The lyrics kept coming back
with images of the guttered fish
and new ones I was learning:

Dolphins leading Roman ships

Cycles are different from circles
The past, unlike the present:
an undulating arc

8

Home again where I was born,
I remembered best the second town
I'd ever lived in

We moved to Henrietta
when I was almost three
We left before I was five

That morning I drank
orange juice and sobbed
but on the trip it rained
on only one side of the road
for a time, I even thought then,
I might be inventing

A tree-house in our yard

Nancy Stine herself had built it for me

Cookies and chickens next door
A hole in the hedge
Movies at the theater
across the vacant lot across the front yard

where once on a walk with my father
I sat down and tried to stand up,
by pulling on my bootstraps,
a feat I'd heard
a worthy man could do

Straining my guts I learned
what the old folks said
was sometimes dumb

And getting pumped to Muddle Lake
where Mountain Boomers were

puffy-throated lizards,
they moved as fast as breath
rising from the hot rocks
they were sailing over

A circus on a neighbor's front porch
A backyard funeral for a goldfish
and I preached the sermon
while someone else took collection
in a grey Homberg hat
Then one day told Skipper Stevenson
that the dimple in his chin
meant the Devil had kissed him,
he was going to Hell

Going home crying
he thought I knew how to read sign

> *Rock of Ages, Satan's cleft,*
> *let me fun myself in thee*

but all I remembered
until 30 years later
was sitting on the curb with him
after breaking some eggs
we stirred in a hole
before we buried the mess
swiped from the henhouse next door

> *and I had a cleft chin, too*
> *He said he'd noticed,*
> *assumed I was different,*
> *my people having power,*
> *my father the preacher and all*

Mrs. Stine's back porch next door,
where the shade gathered breezes,
got painted one day
with dozens of eggs
Chuck, an infant then,
broke on his head
and smeared with his hands
on the red-plank floor

When she found him
he said, "Tookie"
and she gave him one, too

    but probably prayed
    for a dose of restraint

    Ordinarily her lips didn't quiver
    or her temples' veins throb

I was swelling up fat
from breakfast at home
and another next door
until she discovered
my hunger came from something other
than Mother's neglect

    even her Pontiac entertained me:
    parallel chrome lines
    bisecting the trunk,
    and an Indian chief's head on the dash

and her older daughter
named her first son after me
and the other said one cloudy day
that FDR had died

    Nancy Stine knew everything

They and their mother were magic
and also Judge Stine
who taught me to sing
"The Mademoiselle From Armentieres"
and plopped his helmet on my head
while showing me his photographs
of France in World War I

The church by the parsonage,
I was made a life-member
of the Woman's Society (halleluia!)
of Christian Service

but quit crashing choir practice
when a sober man whipped me
with a ping-pong paddle
for singing loud another tune
and playing with the tempting cords
hanging from the ceiling fans

One day I rose from my nap,
took my few clothes off
and joined the church-ladies naked,
unaware of the honor they'd give me

When they finally caught me
they wrapped a dish towel round me
and let me stay—I knew them all
for after church
I'd stand with my father
and greet all the members

it always felt good
to feel a womansoft squeeze

Ours the first family
they'd had in years
with children in it,
and we got taken everywhere

Gladys Dickerson even taught me to drive
by holding me in her lap
while I sputtered enginely
and whipped back and forth
her blue Ford's big steeringwheel

and her husband let me crawl
all over his gigantic tractors

and time after time I charged
house-painting brushes at the lumber yard
catty-corner from the church
though I had to take them back
and get another one,
lying I'd picked out the wrong size

And during church Shorty,
our laughing Sunday cook
who always dressed in white
and wore a great chef's hat,
 tried teaching my brother to jig:
"That boy don't need," he said,
"just to know how to walk
 A man's got to learn how to dance"

9

Cycles in fact are rounder than circles
Cycles in time become globes

breasts and hats
collection plates and tarantula holes
pockets full of surprises
caves and persimmons
pools of water and hills
backs and bellies
hats and fishmouths
the dancing figures bare feet made
bicycle wheels and thought:

cycles of memories turning
through the angled joining-points

creating the flesh of the world
as they did then
in the wishes wind carried
over sidewalk cracks and trees:

triggers for angels and witches,
whimsical baubles jingling
in the driving spasms of dreams

Two Gulls, One Hawk

1

Get right to it, a near voice said:
Say it straight

    No way, I said:
    Crooked's better

Say Being is a tree
whose top twigs touch
the lower reach of heaven

    And be thought a fool?
    Hell, you
    do some listening awhile

    Then the first one said:

Tree and *truth* share a root

    But the second replied:

Not any more

Tree and *true* were the same
From *treow* came *treowth*
and from them *troth*

    Commitment, not Being—
    thrashing is what the tree is

Keep going. Say:
Fidelity's the force
reaching upward
beyond wetness
into light's source

    It stretches downward too

Into inward-turning folds
of earth's moist darkness:
the womanpart of world

That's what I said. So
let gusty breezes
be pageantary and sing:

*Love is the thirst for the eternal
and earth the desert
we stay hungry in*

I wince at the bromides' truth

And I smile at how quotable
the strong sensations of illusion are

There is in breath, in passion
which gives breath speed—

Stop!

Yes? he said, listing

Speed!

Sped at first meant *prosperity*

Sped meant *power*

The two were the same
There is, he said, continuing:
There is in passionate breath
an arm thrown round the knees
of the immortal

Desire appears quickly

Its reception is a seawaving through
the changes of animal breath

Inhaling & exhaling,
no matter if fast
no matter if slow—

As long as a glimmer or murmur of the immortal appears

      Breathing is not dependent on that
      and unity does not last
      in the flesh or in the mind
      The chaos out becomes the chaos in

Unity is a seawaving through troughs and crests

      My desire for its presence,
      its stillness of presence,
      twists me into pain
      When I go into the pit of myself
      I mess up my life

The undulant waves rise and fall
through the rhythms pushing blood
The intimacy you're cast off from comes,
returns when you receive the desire
to be at one with one

      Bring that booger on

Earth and sky join in a grove
A crowd gathers round

      Leave the many in their mobs,
      turning inward in their mobs,
      I want no part of the alien self

      Intimacy, as you call it,
      goes outward too
      That force called lust erupts—

It once meant plainly *desire*

      That force called lust gives blindness sight
      The hell with the many
      I'm craving connection with one

That force called lust erupts . . .

    For out from under feet
    grasshoppers sprayed like omens
    but their sounds were dry,
    a pulmonary clicking,
    bones being rapped in the woods:
    the martyrs were learning new games,
    and I was once a martyr
    sucking at the pit of self
    messing up my life

Reflection and reason—

    Piss on them both

Long ago, in the time before we were,
elders and youth worshipped ancestors

    In dance, in prayer, in play
    We've lost the raunch in rite
    The chaos out: the chaos in

They lit fires whose piquant smoke rose
toward celestial homes

    The earthly ones were too damn confusing
    The young ones rattled the house

The smoke I say rose

    circling above the lower boles
    before disappearing up past the leaves
    into illusion—

Into the sun
which burned marsh dankness
into fragrant mist

Self's swamp still stinks,
no matter how wistful you get

This time, you're right, cannot do the same
We cannot honor ancestors
in the style the old ones used
Ancestors now are only shapes,
names stamped in books by machines

      The old ones, hell, were always names
      Latter-day folklore made them more

The illusion, its truth, made them more

      Don't drone another muttered mass
      The energy of the old ones is useless

Unless we remember them in prayer

      Unless we accept the tensions they bring

But, as you in strain say: Lust erupts

      Winds chap faces
      The winds never rest
      at the point of imbalance
      where we just were
      and are again
      this moment and the next:
      burned to leather on the plains

But when Being—

      Damn you. Listen!
      Seawater laps. New beaches form
      far away from here except in mind
      Fields await our walks

With indifference you think

With vengeance more likely

Only if you maim them

    By god, you're more animistic than I thought

Sounds of grasshoppers return

    The wind
    cool on sweating neck
    comes back

like a song's clear melody

    singing up out of the wreckage of lust

Or do you mean dust?

    The words rising from us
    fall back in new shapes

I hear a rustle in leaves
Is it a serpent?

    Snake, you prig

Or is it a friend?
Or neither one?

    A whistling comes now too

and the image of a lean-to,
the sight of a deer at dawn

    A fawn or a faun?

My eyes, my eyes! They're burning!

2

For a time I wondered why
St. Teresa said she preferred
the monotony of daily labor
to the ecstasies of vision

Soon I knew
the greatest wonder lay
not in her insight
but in our urge
to commemorate strong sensation

Our milder responses, she teaches us,
are perhaps more memorial
than we ever thought
We forget them
We ignored what she said

for there is a thrill
in the maniacal
and another kind of thrill
in cool and listing peace

Sombitch, the third one said:
stillness don't exist
Even your saint knew that
Of course, she had no kids
House apes we used to call them
when we were giving our own parents fits

You're breaking the spell

There is no spell

Live with a kid in a harried time,
try to do something witty
like entertain a vision or two
and more than a spell will break

You must, though, try to sustain
the precious desire for clarity

Live with a kid
in the weather on the plains
and precious desire becomes bald urge

For what?

A flash of connection with one's mate

But there is no stillness

So get on with your truth,
climb that tree you were moaning about

or break a couple of bottles
and fight, it's time we broke
ourselves some skull

The wind today promised
to blow rain here
The sky darkened
but no rain fell
Heat's weight
kept descending upon us
The Dog Days were coming

Dog Days were already here,

and I howled in my heart
but my mouth released no sound

For a time after watering my garden
I sat in a hammock
watching my son and our dog
playing tug-o-war with a sock

My sense of connection with them
was stronger than my invention
of doing the same thing

for I was never a child
who played with his dog
while his father watched

and I, unlike my son,
never had to leave one parent
to live with another

    Hell, you never even had the chance

The drama is not in me, I confess
The drama is somewhere else
I am a fulcrum
Extremes slide toward me
when the stirring winds are right—
I'm sinking into the pit

Perhaps you were never as happy
as he seemed that day

Perhaps your father
never took his fatigue
to a hammock

    He was workin' his butt off
    He didn't hunker down like you

    The past seems like something others had

When you adopt it as your own
you alter it for pleasure,
you alter it for effect

The past does not exist

except as a whimsy of now

or an ache

or an image which allows you to lie about ...

St. Teresa received me into her bosom
Neither one of us knew what to do
though we had a mild laugh
and I helped her sweep the place clean
She thanked me for it
then took a dose
of silence again

She never was known
for being much of a barfighter,
was she? I think not

4

Somewhere in me, prior to blood, antecedent to mind,
in the neural portion of what I am
time blows storms all through me

Dust rushes through trees
Limbs scratch roofs
A horse goes wild with fear
Clouds scud
A funnel comes down: sky's augering whorl

an image of extension:
heaven touching earth
mayhem mayhem mayhem

Just blowin' it all to hell:

The forming of a new shape
caught in the moment of explosion
before the new shape has a story to tell

I am not this night telling stories
I'm listening to my son chatter with my wife
His windy talk wears both of us down
I am not even waiting for a story to form

nor am I telling the truth

Tomorrow morning I shall not go out I think

Lust turns sour when locked in mind's caves

There is too much distraction tonight:
my son chanting, "Santa's coming! Santa's coming!"
out of season
as he brings in the kitten
in a pillowcase
and drops it on the floor

along with a load of chatter
he piles upon the desk

How can I descend into the coals of ancient fires?
How can I do anything but drink myself to sleep?
The distractions are exposing how vacant I am

You're fighting the vagrant self
Your son's more interesting than
a celibate, broom-wielding nun

Earlier tonight I saw the moon
A cross was flowing from it
but I couldn't remember
what the sign meant

All day I'd felt gut-sick,
bitter that my flesh
was only worth sticks—
I craved an odalisque

Or St. Teresa?

The cross reminded me
of someone spread-eagled
Clouds soon came
and covered her up, or the moon

You were only fighting self
for no good purpose

Your dog was panting
and so were you,
and I wasn't far from being out of breath myself

How can I descend now into ancient fires?
How can I do anything but drink myself to sleep
and rue the fact that St. Teresa's mind
is (or was?) more even-paced than mine

5

Think of the others,
the ones fanning scribbles into meager flames the timid laud
You have read their mewlings about their own mortality

    In planar, unbardic fashion they scratch
    with affectations of an absent mask

       Their mouths are dry lagoons

And a bird—perhaps a scissortail,

       though they call it swallow in their gay way—

fans off the hawk
it was pestering awhile ago

The field you crossed to go fishing that day
was patched with rabbit droppings,
but only grasshoppers fled from your feet
Stickers clung to your pants and shoelaces,
pricked your skin through your socks

The morning was hot. For awhile
you thought you'd missed morning feeding,
then the bites started coming, but then eased off—

      There would be no yarn to tell

You hooked nothing big enough
to give a yearner a fine vicarious thrill
There was time, there was heat,
there were ordinary aggravations
of temper and unrest caused by illusions of distance:

      the lyrical urge fractured by self

Only goddern real image
was the lake you were gonna get muddy in—
no grits, no peppers, no pussy, not even
a fried potater

Some friends you knew, you later discovered,
were going through sickness and death
You were sobered by their grief
Your hands went to their shoulders
as you awkwardly passed through their doors

Their agonies won't stir the world

But you know their pain, the shrieks bursting from them
A power is marking their lives with a scar
that they wear better than you wear yours

Don't forget, if you're courting despair,
the old Sioux death-chant, friend:
Our friend and brother's dead
Let's gather by the fire
and smoke the tobacco he left

If you could make friends with that idea
you could make friends with freedom

and blow the dank world into fire,
into a firestorm
burning self to ash

Only the spirit of form would remain
You could build a world from it—

If I committed myself to an arcane lie

Too much wit'll just tucker you out

6

Be still be still be still
It's lullaby time

I don't want to be still
I've got a craving to thrash

But you aren't acting on it
You rarely do
You'd rather bitch about your odalisque

Your fantasy, not mine
My anger comes
when playful moves I've made
are grinned at in her distance

Her rhythms are slower than yours
Her rhythms have always been
ready to sing with yours

That I'm not denying

So get off your ass and act
if action's what you want

The moon last night was full,
its color white
like the mercury vapor light
on the street corner

An icy wind was blowing
slivers of chill through cracks by the door
Dogs began howling
when the air grew still

And you?

I, I'm saying, am the dogs

Then your rhythms are really much slower than hers,
quite slower than hers

    The question is really not speed

Oh it is
Power is what you're railing about:
the satisfaction of the fantasies you crave
when you're sitting hunkered on your ass
Go work your garden—your weeds are yourself

      No, I said, refusing to submit
      to the fleshless ghost
      of another new dream

        St. Teresa dancing with her broom
        St. Teresa stripteasing him

Then what does she do after that display?
What does she do to entertain you then?

      I'm sinking
      It's not a battle of wits I want

Then what?

      An end to the banter,
      a blossoming of lust
      Once it burst repeatedly
      then reflection set in
      and clothed desire

It wasn't reflection,
or even the kid,
his rowdiness in your nest

      I never said it was, I lied

You're lazy
You want the dream to come to you

    I do
    Would you like more coffee?

I suppose you think it's a crime
the time's not right for wine

7

Little was stable in the weather they lived in

Winds howled like cats gone mad
erratically in all four seasons
Sun shone in the cold
and in heat clouds teased the sky
with dreams of rain which rarely came
The ground was hard red clay
Its surface rolled
as if explosions under earth
could not break topsoil loose

Across the river and north
craggy mountains bluffed
West of them the desert began
and the sea was even more distant
Grandeur rolled around them
but farther away than eye could see—
their place a spokeless, huge wheel's hub
obliquely rolled by the mob
whose own surfaces rolled
as if explosions under earth
could not break topsoil loose

The place was its own rough weather
and they were the rhythms of lyrical strain
when capricious winds' dust sang
>   *Winds are gods*
>   *and gods are wind*
>   *mayhem mayhem mayhem*

She had been a vagabond,
swamp born. Her home became the world
Home was the place she nestled in
but nestling and nesting are not the same

>   Intending rape, boys had told her and her friends:
>   *Pass me you tongue, Bébé*
>   *I'm hot for you, Sha*

Rejecting them and choosing him, she accepted his place,
its expansive stretch of peaceful illusion,
the craggy wildness called the plains
where indirection is ribald play
as well as flint-eyed sober truth

The only dry thing she'd seen as a child
was spanish moss hanging from oaks
The only wet thing he'd seen
throbbed and writhed in distant dreams
Bayous' dankness rolled near her
Her mind rose out of that cloying place

His, though, went toward the swamps
           Pass me you tongue, Bébé
but the habit of wryness made him laugh

Her body sang richly with her dreams
and she was at least as oblique as he
Serpents had writhed close to her eyes
Serpents had even licked her lips
but she was not afraid of them

He was
though he defied his fear

           but defiance rarely sings
           unless you laugh and embrace the noise
           and lie your way back toward the truth

Snakes to her were curling things
graceful in the vines
and lazy mid the stench of muddy banks

Snakes to him were lethal shocks
anxious to spring from under rocks

The clay and swamp rose round them

8

You mentioned the gods
I've heard you do that before
Do you really believe they exist
or are you tossing dice
into figures of speech?

    Such as snake-eyes,
    a pitiless image of live wire-ends?

No

    Gods do exist

How?

    I prefer not to say

You're hedging
Call them Being and be direct

    The I-Am-That-I-Am, the notion of
    the motion of the world
    which speaks itself?

I said you're hedging
The question was mine

    Are Love and Justice one?
    Is Being the body achieving grace?

        Whose body do you mean
        and which of its parts?

All of them
The moisture in the flesh,
the force in the wetness
defying for a time
the flesh going dry

And that you call the gods?

     Yes. If you'll let the phrase be
     God is god-the-gods

I think you mean the muscular truth of illusion

     Fine. Stories and talk have flesh
     They, like the gods, are that within
     which is also beyond us

You haven't really answered me

     Of course not
     You're casting for direction yourself

Answer me!

     I have
     You asked if I believed in gods
     I told you yes

You never said why

     I did though

When?

     When both of us saw
     St. Teresa pushing her broom
     There's glory in that
     and a clean floor too

But the spectacle's mute
There has to be some spectacle
at the moment the gods are named,
for they are the force turning the world,
and the act of naming should shine
In what you've said the spectacle's mute

It's not if you know how to look
In the room where she swept
a light came through a thin window
Its slant spilled down on the floor
Motes of dust sparkled
Inhaling them she was drawing
heaven's earthfire into herself

But she kept sweeping

She had a task to do
Knowledge of it lifted her up

Beyond her arms and legs?

Through the flesh of arms and legs

Serenely?

At times. Not every time
Sometimes our shadows smother her fire
Sometimes we forget to continue to sweep

But the floor will never stay clean

Why should it?
It's moving with the earth
through the stars

9

Cold, the mountains rose keenly
past tumbleweeds and prickly pear
My attention rose with them,
rose beyond the purple mounds
into cloud-ribboned waters of sky

And boulder-like clouds

Above the rocks: an ocean,
a waveless expanse of blue
so still it seemed to lack depth,
so far away no term of distance
could name it, but I was rising
into it. Rock peaks pointed the way

The rocks were thunderheads

But the cords in my neck began straining
My attention was falling back down
into the ground I was planted on

I knew no vision would come that day

The sun was baking my shoulders and face
The scorching heat reminded me
there had been no dancers and music,
no congregants making spectacle,
no community to turn the illusion
of reaching toward liquidity
into undulant truth. I was alone

Around me were tumbleweed and prickly pear,
the smell of basil and dill in a tended place,
and the clouds forming above me
rose into pale islands, became voluptuous flesh
forlorn and pale in a wave-breaking sea—

Stop!
If you had stayed out through night
you would have seen stars passing,
gathering in images from all the seasons
You would have been able to trace
old stories sketched in their patterns
You would have seen them disappear,
felt a breeze stirring around you,
you would have been bathed by a rain

and if you had not moved,
the animals of your desert's edge
would have gathered at your feet
and stayed there until, at dawn,
you began seeing the far mountains
changing from purple to red, then to brown
For a moment yellow would have splashed them

        Another droll dream
        Mountains can't be seen from here

You would have seen them,
then the rattlesnakes and jackrabbits,
field mice, the grackles and lizards—
all the creatures resting by your feet—
would come awake, go back to war and flight

        Some of them would not survive,
        heavy-footed as you are

Their blood would stain your boots
Feathers, hair and gut-clots would stick
to your trouserlegs

        And a fire would sweep
        with grief and joy all around you

But your own flesh would not burn
What would have happened might happen yet

And might not too
Nothing's sure at desert's edge

I went back again the next day

Where?

To the water where the fish are

But you went there alone

I didn't

You simply woke up

I wanted to try again to rise
into the wetness of sky

By slushing through mud?

I wanted completeness:
lyrical song, muscular wit

But you went there alone

I wanted to taste the wet sky,
feel its ooze sliding upon me,
take in my hands and mouth
the soft texture of its mounding flesh

But you went there alone

I was burned again by the sun
Its weight prevented my flight
from rising beyond the depthless sky
into its unseen folds, into its voice

No. Into its meat
Quit euphemizing lust

I'm not

But you went there alone,
yet even if you had risen that far,
if you had risen into the textures promised by dreams
you would have drifted bewildered back to clay,
for a vision is an irrelevant thing
unless the mating, which is what you're talking about,
takes place with another,
takes place in the dust on the ground

>   Swamp, mountains, plains
>   Sweat mingling with flesh
>   and musk-fragrant hair

>   But the dry heat burned my big bones brittle

You went there alone
Forget the sticks described by mind
They only nail your tongue
and gnarl your leathery flesh

10

Don't bring St. Teresa into this

He wasn't

Accept a moment of stillness,
even if you have to invent it
There's a blessing where you live

A blessed rumbling in my gut

What does that have to do with the mob?

Nothing
I didn't even mention the mob,
the fretting that they bring

Good. So let us now perform a miracle
or break a couple beer bottles and fight

You've turned droll yourself
It's been a long time since you even came close
to laying open a head or two

We need no valley. The plains will do fine

But you do need a mob
For a miracle there must be a crowd
You've said so yourself
A vision might be private
You can have one of those in a closet
but for a big blowout of a mass
you need a mob

I was speaking of miracles, not theatrics,
but go ahead and bring the folks on

Can't. They're out fooling around
They follow their urges
better than I follow mine

Or if not better
then certainly more often
Chewing the fat means more than *talking*

I doubt it,
but bring them on I say. It's time
we performed a miracle,
it's time to blow the wind away

Are you the one
now making light
of the urge in the flesh for the sacred?

I said we need a miracle here

Then perform that thing
I'm losing myself in the labyrinth of self
My legs are becoming concrete

Damnit, get it going before he busts

I am

When?

Soon. In a moment if you'll hush

I probably won't
and neither will my son who wants to be
the *genius loci* of this house

He's as anarchic as you,
only his demons brawl
all over the surface,
but your demons clot
before they reach flesh

So what do you need?

Attention and quiet

> You have my attention
> but I won't be quiet
> My feet are locked in clay

>> Just don't bitch about it
>> the rest of the day

Let your mind soar

> Be serious. A story first

>> I knew a woman
>> She wanted a buzzard for a pet,
>> finally caught one too,
>> but the bald-headed thing
>> threw up its dinner in her lap

You're trying to distract me
Making things hard for me
you make them rough on yourself

> No, I'm not. I knew her too
> She wanted a buzzard
> She caught one too
> and also snared a hawk
> which pecked her lynx-eyes blind

>> Poor lady had no liver
>> Her ancestors were the ones with guts

You and your carrion mind

> No. Once again you've missed the point
> The sober one often does
> My legs are turning light again

You think you should throw yourself into drunkenness then?

No. A minor fit of an ecstasy will do

Then what?

    I want to see your miracle
    I want to see you perform it

        We need a spasm of distraction here

Gather the wood for the fire

    We're out of oak

Mesquite will do fine

    It's already stacked

Light it

    Done

Observe the flames
Can you see yourself in them?

    No

What do you see?

    The flesh of the wood going to smoke

And the heat waving off wood,
heat shimmering before smoke forms

    I see it

Look deeper and see yourself

    You're not speaking of omens, are you?

No

You can't see yourself in a fire
The shapes that dance there
are more entertaining than self
They're lighter than limbs and hotter than loins

So what do you see?

Shapes having themselves a damn fine time

Can't you try to be serious?

I could, but when I do
my guts knot up

That means you're approaching the point
where a spirit desires to get loose

Don't let it
You don't know what it might do
You don't know where it's been
The pit of self's a mess

Ride the tension out

No sense in that

Ride it out, your body's free
and Being is an impressive tree

Just cut the crap and let me see
a miracle performed mostly for me

Create an angelus
Smite that dandy
hip and thigh

Hush! What do you see?

In the fire is an ocean
The flame-spits are waves
Orange cloaks dance
but red ones slip away,
blue-green ones flee
A yellow spurt flashes
Dusts of ashes are grey

Don't look so hard at the ashes
Listen awhile. What do you hear?

Sticks cracking in heat,
boiling sap whistling,
a distant wind, heat gusts
and clicking—

Do you know where the clicking's from?

No

It comes with the memories of grasshoppers
flying out from under your feet,
but don't fix on the fishing you've done
Let an image come to you
Watch that image formed by fire
What does it want to be?

He gives up, you keep the prize

If not a cicada,
whatever I want

Relax your damn will
Let it, like smoke, drift away
The image—what image did you see?

I was working alone in the garden
My wife appeared at my side
Our arms, as if unbodied,
went around us. We kissed
Our thoughts grew into flesh
Our thoughts were in our hands

They were dancing in your thighs
and in your shaking bellies

Juice inside a peach,
the power of its stain
as sweet and tart as its sensual taste

Go on

Sometimes when I prune my trees
I give away the sticks
Friends get them for kindling
Sometimes, though, I save those sticks
for gardenstakes,
but often I lose them
or throw them away

Let the image come
then throw those sticks as far as you can
Listen to them hum

They're boomerangs

The miracle has begun

11

The sand of the sea shifts under your feet
A gull flies inland toward desert
Its mate waits for it there

The fruit of the prickly pear's turned red

The gulls fly together,
their feathers the colors of clouds

A hawk sweeps a circle above them

The gulls do not know it's there
They fly together till twilight comes

The hawk's now in a leafless tree,
but buds on twigs are beginning to form
The frost in the weather of self is past

And without sound the sun
throws the low clouds into explosion:
red orange yellow violet—
opulence now and radiance too

The fire the tree the gods

The gulls come to rest on the sand

All night the flint-eyed hawk
keeps vigil above them

To protect them or attack them?

Tonight no rattler will strike through their sleep
You and your kind will dream, if you dream,
of green valleys, troughs in the sea,
and the range of mountains liquidly rising above them
The hawk will need no dream
The hawk's eyes cut through night
as yours might do

And in the morning when dew glistens flowers

When dew shines crowns-of-thorns and prickly pear,

When mica and quartz catch the sun in sandstone

the hawk will no longer be in the tree
but flying away, in the distance now,
he'll hold in his talons
the power of darkness he's seized from the land

And the gulls will leave to look for a lake,
waves from a thousand mirages glowing below them

Is phosphorous in the desert's sea?

And have you heard the clicking yet?

From grasshoppers or rattlesnakes?
Or from the bones Ezekiel knew?

Or the cracking of waves Amos heard
when justice rolled like a torrent?

You have in your hand a long stick
You won't need it for a weapon
or for walking today
You'll throw it as far as you can
but it won't leave your hand
You'll throw it again as far as you can
but it won't leave your hand

The stick itself is my hand

And the thrust in your arm?

The animate drive of lyrical form,
my body extending communicantly

You understand now
the patterns driving will into
breath into will beyond self

    This stick is the weather
    I hold in my hands

Lightning and breezes, sunlight and shade,
the rage to sail clear through mountainous waves

    The sky's turning red
    The blood of god slain
    spreads through the sky

But the tint comes from dust

    It always has

Where I ask is the miracle?

    There wasn't one

        Jacklegged jokes chased it away

There was. A miracle did occur

    No. It didn't
    unless you conjure back the moment
    you in your whimsy invented
    when tree became truth:

    the tubular stick in St. Teresa's hand

        a concentration on
        a contraction in the groin
        when she squeezed it—
        I heard a fine moan

and love transformed the lust to prayer

    and prayer became erotic desire

The gasp of sunset leaving

    She leaned hard upon her broom

Be still now, still

    The moon will sweep the night away

The darkest part of night remains, be still

    In memory it stays
    though moon's light shines:
    a frozen fire

        burning the self-clotted pall of clouds away

And the trees' fingers reach

    For what?

The floor of the heavens

    hair and flesh of god-the-gods

And the arms of the other you complete yourself with

    But the wind—
    It's rising again

The wind is your breath and her breath joined
and, freed, the breath returns then slides
between your bellies, up your thighs
and moisture sprays from ocean waves
rising and troughing

    in your undulant
    and shrimp-scented hair

    The gulls and the hawk—
    They're flying now

Your arms will sail on past them

    My wife was with me there in the garden
    A throbbing in my loins,
    a fluttering through our flesh

As wind begins dying
love's shudder retrieves it

    But where is the flame
    that colored the clouds?

In the throbbing you touch and redeem yourselves with:
the embracement that's vaster than self,

    the joy transcending rage and spite,
    the gladness of pleasure
    and freedom from self

        Self's the pissantedness of our time,
        a waste of flesh
        a muddlement of mind
        Spit into the wind
        and the wind spits back

But you were right
There was no miracle,
not today, no miracle came

    But in her eyes a radiance shone

That was then
St. Teresa's now alone

    She's not, and besides
    she's not the one I meant

In the form of a breeze god-
the-gods winnowed her hair
We all were there
She was our Other

She's not the one I meant

Yet she kept on sweeping around you
You had left the naked sun,
the scorcht place in your grove
You had left the breezeless dark
pressing heavily upon you

We watched her,
uncovered head bowed,
blessing the floor

As night came sleep came with it

And with sleep dreams

Of what?

We were lying below her high window
in the long moist grass

And a miracle, you think, occurred?

The hawk disappeared
The gulls were gone too
A light came over the land
As I opened my eyes I remembered—

Say it

I can't
The taste of blood and salt is on my tongue

The mark of god slain

Wine-redness of dawn

Then a shaft of a shadow came down
from the high thin window where no glass was
A breeze passed over you

Its coolness covered us
The grass beneath us
became again green,
was no longer straw

A miracle did occur
There were others embraced by that shadow
They knew it though you were unmindful of them
For a moment a miracle did light upon you
and it touched them too

But they'll forget
They always do

Our arms around our backs,
we pressed together
Our arms for a moment curled
all around the whirl-drunk world,
and the heat of our touching
is still fast upon us

Love does that, and wine,
the blessings of her
tending cloister for you

We rose through distractions,
past confusions of fatigue
Redemption came

It comes from pushing your dust
into form

Our sweat dripped upon it
and the dirt took shape

It was her sweat as much as yours
and tears as much as sweat

They come from the trouble children bring,
from the shafts of the shadows
we imagine they cast between us—

The distractions of their irreverent force

Children lie within us all
In darkness a memory of light
shines wanly in our eyes

Why wanly?

The world read St. Teresa's story wrong,
and we when we're harried
do the same with our own
The grief of the inner, self-locked wind

The hawk near the gulls again

The world lying moistly,
its matting our bed

And the dawn rose into noon
that descended to dusk
whose sunset gasped into night

But lightning brought the twilight heaving back

Then darkness caved in upon us
yet dawn, like a wedge, stirred again up through it

The slow undulation of time
moving around you
and waving through your flesh
You took up her broom

Blest by the burden you felt
your arms going light
Such happens in memory more than flight

And by it we measure the rhythms of time

That's surely your mistake, not hers
She took her broom back, and sweeping
she accepted the visions when they came
She did not demand a new one each day
She said she preferred—

       Her preference is not mine
       She had no child and loved no mate
       though Christ in her found flesh

But you can't reject her

       I'm not
       Her knowledge begins the past
       of what our lyrical miracle is
       A shining tone rings
       beyond the noise
       coming from the lungs
       but barely reaching tongue—

              Except in rage or praise,
              except in whimsies of speech

But what about that volcanic pit
you called the howling bowels of self?

       Battered, I measured worlds by it
       But when our arms curl now
       around the whirl-drunk world
       we are lying together
       beyond that world,
       we are standing together
       within that world
       and my son is seeing it with us

Two gulls, one hawk
soaring through the vagrant light

And a stillness shines beyond you
over the earth and down into soil

deeply into the fragrant earth
and out through a radiance of distant stars

Their huge spread of light
touches this place where we are.

James Hoggard is a native of Wichita Falls, Texas, where he has taught at Midwestern University since 1966. As a novelist, short fictionist, playwright, poet, essayist, and translator, Hoggard has published widely in such magazines as *Southwest Review*, *Partisan Review*, *Redbook*, and *Beyond Baroque 691*. Most recently he has published a non-fiction work, *Elevator Man* (E-Heart Press), as well as *The Shaper Poems* (Cedarshouse Press). A novel, *Trotter Ross*, was issued in 1981 by Thorp Springs Press and in 1977 Trilobite Press brought out a group of his poems entitled *Eyesigns*. A member of the Texas Institute of Letters and in 1979 the recipient of an NEA writers fellowship, Hoggard has remained throughout his career a chameleon of literary forms, an experimentalist working with every genre after his own regional manner.